NO
YORKSHIRE
DOG FRIENDLY
PUB WALKS

PETER NALDRETT

COUNTRYSIDE BOOKS
NEWBURY BERKSHIRE

First published 2021
© 2021 Peter Naldrett

COUNTRYSIDE BOOKS
3 Catherine Road
Newbury, Berkshire

To view our complete range of books please visit us at
www.countrysidebooks.co.uk

ISBN 978 1 84674 400 6

All materials used in the manufacture of this book carry FSC certification

Produced by The Letterworks Ltd., Reading
Designed and Typeset by KT Designs, St Helens
Printed by Holywell Press, Oxford

Contents

Walk

INTRODUCTION

From the waves crashing on the North Sea coastline to the lofty summits of hills in the Pennines, the landscape of North Yorkshire is as varied as anywhere in the country. It's a county where you can be enjoying fish and chips on the seafront one day after a stroll along Whitby's Cinder Trail and then the day after enjoy a strenuous climb up the iconic Roseberry Topping to enjoy a far-reaching view across the moors. This varied and exciting landscape has an incredible array of adventures for any curious dog and it's been a pleasure to collect 20 of my favourite dog walks in this book. Of course, it's not just about the dogs having a good time – we also want the humans in the party to make the most of the day. And to that end, each of the walks has a dog friendly pub to go with it. Having a pub that welcomes dogs is crucial to many people when planning a day out. Not only is it somewhere they can let their dog rest after a long run around, it's also somewhere the owners can unwind in friendly, welcoming surroundings and make sure they have some good food and drink to round the day off. It'll come as no surprise that I've really enjoyed sampling the delights of the food and drink menu in some of these pubs, and I can say that you're in for a real treat.

Each of the walks in this North Yorkshire collection has been planned with the dog owner in mind. They follow a range of different paths, including some well-known and much-loved long-distance trails, wind along farm tracks, mirror former train lines and call in at delightful villages. There's even the chance to explore the solar system and take a trip out to Pluto! The walks are intended to give you and your dog as much off-lead time as possible, cut down on the number of stiles and make sure that you always have the details of a nearby vet close at hand. Many of the walks skirt by rivers and enter woodland, enhancing the experience for your beloved pet. It's not possible, of course, to visit the best areas in the Yorkshire Dales and the North York Moors and have 100% off-lead time. By definition, our National Parks are home to wild areas of nesting birds and farms rearing livestock, so at all times an element of responsibility is needed to protect these special landscapes and those who we share them with. This responsibility extends to using leads when necessary, clearing up after your dog and sharing the trails sensibly with other users. While many of the paths are well-used and in very good condition, make sure you're always wearing sturdy footwear and dress according to the weather. Take an Ordnance Survey map with you, plan the route ahead and make sure you have plenty of charge on your phone. Being fully prepared for a day out in the countryside – where the weather can turn on a sixpence – always makes for a better day out for both you and your dog.

There is so much scope for having adventurous days out walking the paths of North Yorkshire, enjoying the splendour of the Yorkshire Dales, North York Moors and all the area in between. Whether you're looking for fun in the countryside or places to base yourself for weekends away, I hope this book helps you out and plants the seed that grows your love of this part of the world.

Thanks to Nicola, Toby, Willow and Neil for joining me on these delightful walks.

Peter Naldrett

PUBLISHER'S NOTE

We hope that you and your dog obtain considerable enjoyment from this book; great care has been taken in its preparation. In order to assist in navigation to the start point of the walk, we have included the nearest postcode, however, a postcode cannot always deliver you to a precise starting point, especially in rural areas. Although at the time of publication all routes followed public rights of way or permitted paths, diversion orders can be made and permissions withdrawn.

We cannot, of course, be held responsible for such diversion orders or any inaccuracies in the text which result from these or any other changes to the routes, nor any damage which might result from walkers trespassing on private property. We are anxious, though, that all the details covering the walks are kept up to date, and would therefore welcome information from readers which would be relevant to future editions.

The simple sketch maps that accompany the walks in this book are based on notes made by the author whilst surveying the routes on the ground. They are designed to show you how to reach the start and to point out the main features of the overall circuit, and they contain a progression of numbers that relate to the paragraphs of the text.

However, for the benefit of a proper map, we do recommend that you purchase the relevant Ordnance Survey sheet covering your walk – details of the relevant sheet are with each walk.

It's also wise to check at the bar that there is no problem leaving your car in the pub car park before or after your visit.

ADVICE FOR DOG WALKERS

The Countryside Code lists six steps to ensure your walk in the countryside is as safe as possible. These are:

1 Keep your dog on a lead, or in sight at all times, be aware of what it's doing and be confident it will return to you promptly on command.

2 Ensure it does not stray off the path or area where you have a right of access.

3 When using access rights over open countryside and common land you must keep your dog on a short lead between 1 March and 31 July, to help protect ground-nesting birds, and all year round near farm animals.

4 Keep your dog on a lead around farm animals, particularly sheep, lambs and horses. This is for your own safety and for the welfare of the animals. A farmer may shoot a dog which is attacking or chasing farm animals without being liable to compensate the dog's owner.

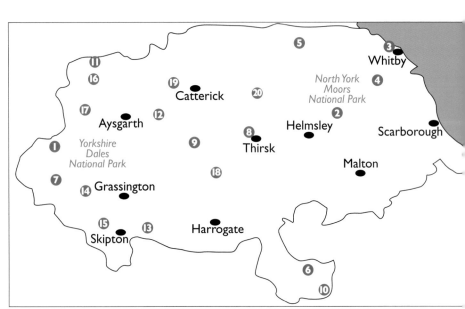

Area map showing location of the walks

5 However, if cattle or horses chase you and your dog, it is safer to let your dog off the lead – don't risk getting hurt by trying to protect it. Your dog will be much safer if you let it run away from a farm animal in these circumstances and so will you.

6 Everyone knows how unpleasant dog mess is and it can cause infections, so always clean up after your dog and get rid of the mess responsibly – 'bag it and bin it'. Make sure your dog is wormed regularly to protect it, other animals and people.

Please show a sensible attitude when encountering other walkers, dog owners, sheep, cows and cyclists.

1 RIBBLEHEAD
3 miles (5.2 km)

One of the most iconic sights of the Yorkshire Dales, the gorgeous Ribblehead Viaduct is a testimony to the brilliance of Victorian engineering and their determination to lay a railway through the harsh landscape towards Carlisle. Enjoy a visit to the pub at the local station and stretch your legs and your dog's on the path alongside the railway, looping around to pass beneath one of the famous arches. This is one of the most photographed places in the country and it's worth hanging around until a train passes over the top of the viaduct to make your snaps extra special. You can even leave the car at home for this route and make your way to Ribblehead train station.

Start & Finish: Ribblehead Viaduct Car Park, Blea Moor Road.
Sat Nav: LA6 3AS.
Parking: Free parking is available close to the junction between the B6479 and the B6255 that meet here.
OS Map: OS Explorer 2 Yorkshire Dales Southern & Western Areas.
Grid ref: SD765793.

THE PUB

THE STATION INN is well known as the pub next to the viaduct and many walkers call in for a pint after tackling the local hills. The pub itself has a rich history, dating back to the 1870s and opening up around the same time as the viaduct. Initially, the business doubled up as both a farm and pub

– a working tradition that continued until the 1960s. Dogs are welcome at the pub, where you'll find a real sense of history and a place proud of its industrial heritage. When the railway was being constructed, there were up to 2000 workers living in these remote surroundings, with the makeshift settlements given marvellous names such as Jericho, Jerusalem and Sebastopol. The 24 arches are quite something, but the human cost was high. Around 100

people died making the viaduct, which is just one of several carrying the railway along the 72-mile journey from Settle to Carlisle.
☎ 01524 241274 ⊕ thestationinnribblehead.com

Terrain: Well established paths.
Livestock: Sheep may be encountered on farming fields. There is off-lead time between the viaduct and the starting point.
Stiles: No stiles.
Nearest vet: Dalehead Veterinary Group, 22 Station Road, Settle, BD24 9AA. ☎ 01729 823538 ⊕ daleheadvetgroup.co.uk

---

The Walk

. . . .

1 Whether you're starting from the parking place or the train station, make your way to the path a little way down the hill from the pub and begin to head out towards the viaduct. It's signed towards Whernside, the large hill you can see beyond the viaduct that makes up one of the Yorkshire Three Peaks. As you reach the brow of the hill on the way to the famous arches, it's a good place to take in the view and get a photo – not just of the viaduct but of the whole panorama.

2 When you get down towards the viaduct, take the path that leads off to the right rather than going on the main route beneath the arch. Again, there is a sign for Whernside, and the path mirrors the route of the railway, steadily rising until you're almost on a level with it. Follow this path for just over ½ mile.

3 The path drops down into a little dip, and then you

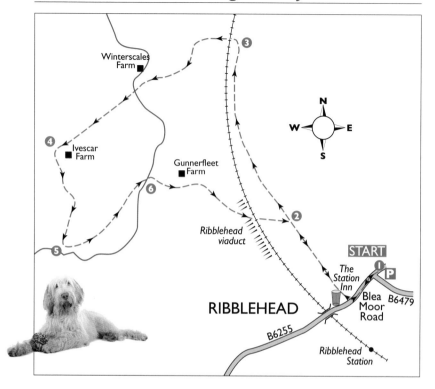

reach a path to the left beneath the track. Take this passageway that takes you beneath the railway line, following the path on the other side that runs across the fields. It's a simple path to follow as it takes you over farmland. You'll walk through Winterscales Farm, where there's a lovely section with limestone drystone walls. Keep on the main path and make sure you admire the unique outline of Ingleborough over to the left.

4 You'll reach the next farm, Ivescar, in just over ¼ mile. When you reach it you need to take the path off to the left and walk between the buildings. This is a simple section of the route, easy to follow on good terrain.

5 As the main farm track bends around to the right, leave it by taking the track off to the left. You'll now be crossing over several fields and heading towards another farm building. Keep ahead for just over ¼ mile.

6 Before you reach the next farm, take the path off to the right. Walk past the farm buildings – which are on your left – and follow the route as it heads towards the dominating viaduct. Keep to the main path as it passes underneath one of the 24 arches. At the other side there are boulders on the ground, and from here you turn right and retrace your steps back to the road.

2 HUTTON-LE-HOLE
4½ miles (7.3 km)

The return leg of this circular 4½-mile walk is simply delightful, covering Spaunton escarpment and enjoying the magnificent views across the valley. Elsewhere, you'll be passing through rural fields, walking down a few country lanes and tackling farming tracks in a range of environments for your dog to explore. There are plenty of stunning landscapes to keep you entertained for an afternoon along this lovely walk from the village. It may be worth planning to spend the day around Hutton-le-Hole, however. The village is one of the best-looking in the country and is a jewel in this part of North Yorkshire. There's also an open air museum telling the story of local heritage and culture.

Start & Finish: Moor Lane, Hutton-le-Hole. **Sat Nav: YO62 6UA.**
Parking: Pay and display car park on Moor Lane in the centre of Hutton-le-Hole.
OS Map: OS Explorer OL 26: North York Moors, Western Area.
Grid ref: SE705902.

THE PUB

THE CROWN in Hutton-le-Hole, with its exposed beams and a menu that is guaranteed to get you excited, makes for a superb addition on your day out in the North York Moors. Time your walk to coincide with a meal-time and you can take advantage of a menu that favours local produce and has a whole range of favourites to choose from – from fish and chips to steak pie, and topped off with a sticky toffee pudding. There are many other walks to set out on around Hutton-le-Hole, meaning that you might fancy basing yourself in the pub for a night or two. The accommodation is dog friendly, and if you're here for the evening you might want to get involved in the pub quiz or one of the other events run by the pub. Camping and caravan fans will be pleased to know there is space to pitch your tent and take advantage of an electrical hook-up at the rear of the pub.

☎ 01751 417343 ⊕ crownhuttonlehole.com

Terrain: Well established paths that climb gentle slopes. Small amount of road walking.
Livestock: Sheep may be encountered on farming fields. Observe local signs, especially on the moorland.
Stiles: No stiles.
Nearest vet: Grace Lane Vets, Weighbridge Close, Kirkbymoorside, YO62 6FD. ☎ 01751 432777⊕ gracelanevets.com

The Walk

❶ From the car park, turn left and head down Moor Lane. At the main road turn left past the pub, and head along the road in the middle of the village towards the church. Take the public footpath signed on the left which you'll find on the far side of the church. This will take you into an open field and soon you'll pass through a small wood. The path is easy to follow during this section and in ½ mile you'll be brought out at a small country road (Anserdale Lane).

2 At the road, turn right and follow it for about ½ mile. Just before you reach a bridge, take the path heading off to the left and follow it as it bends around to the right. With the moorland on your left, this track will take you ¼ mile beyond Camomile Farm and bring you out at a junction of paths.

3 Turn right here and head into Lastingham, which is another fine Yorkshire village. At the junction in the centre of Lastingham, turn left and continue along the road (Front Street). At the next junction, take the turning on the right and head across the bridge over a small stream.

4 When you reach a farm building in 100 metres, take the path on the right. This part of the walk takes you up a steepish hill and through another small wood, giving your dog a great chance to explore some of the scents around the trees.

5 When you get to Oldfield Lane, turn right onto it. Continue along the straight section of the road (now Hallings Lane) and follow it around a tight turn to the right. Shortly after the turn, take the path on the left following the signs guiding you through Grange Farm. There's a right and a left turn to take before you leave the farm.

6 The path heading away from Grange Farm back towards

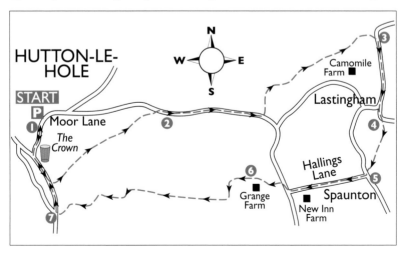

Hutton-le-Hole is well marked and after an initial straight section there will be a left and then a right turn to make. A long, straight section takes you across several fields before the paths starts to descend towards the village, making a left and right turn and then following the path down through a wood. This takes you down the hill and you'll spend some of the time walking next to a stream, which is a good place for those with four legs to have a paddle.

❼ On reaching the road, turn right and head back into Hutton-le-Hole towards the pub and car park.

3 HAWSKER & WHITBY
6 miles (9.6 km)

A **fantastic there-and-back dog walk** that's on the level and enjoys a few sea views, there's a lot to be said for taking off to the Cinder Track for the day. This former railway line was converted to a recreational path when the old lines were torn up and today is a very popular route to let dogs off the lead for a run around. When the walk reaches Whitby at the halfway point, there's an option to extend the walk and head down into the famous coastal town. Maybe there'll even be time to treat yourself to fish and chips? Walking part of this much-loved track – which connects Whitby with Scarborough further down the coast – will leave you wanting to discover more of it and ensure you and your dog return.

Start & Finish: The Hare & Hounds, Hawsker.
Sat Nav: YO22 4LH.
Parking: Street parking is available in the village of Hawsker, close to the pub.
OS Map: OL27 North York Moors Eastern Area.
Grid ref: NZ927075.

THE PUB **THE HARE & HOUNDS** at Hawsker is a traditional pub which at the same time has a contemporary feel, and has the right combination of ales and good food to make it well worth a visit after the walk. The menu has an emphasis on local produce and seasonal variations. There will be a warm welcome for you and your dog and you can rest assured that the bar area is designated dog friendly. Because of its proximity to the popular coastal trail, you can expect to see plenty of walkers and cyclists enjoying a stop-off here. ☎ 01947 880453 ⊕ hareandhoundshawsker.co.uk

Terrain: Accessible route along a former railway line.
Livestock: None.
Stiles: No stiles.
Nearest vet: Clevedale Vets, The Parade, Whitby, YO21 3JP.
☎ 01947 825042 ⊕ clevedalevets.co.uk

The Walk

- -

1 Starting in Hawsker, close to the Hare and Hounds pub, head down the B1447 road until you reach the Methodist Chapel at the junction with the A171. Turn right towards Whitby and walk on the path beside this busy road. In 200 metres you'll reach the Cinder Track as the road starts to bend round to the left.

2 Take the turning for the Cinder Track on the left, walking towards Whitby. This is where the fun times start for your dog. There are no stiles, the route is enclosed and you won't come across any livestock, so it's off-lead time all the way from here. There are trees and long grasses for your dog to explore and you're sure to come across one or two other dogs for them to make friends! The track leaves the route of the main road immediately and takes you past the back of some houses before heading out to a tree-lined route with countryside beyond.

3 In ¾ mile, before approaching the village of Stainsacre, the track bends a little to the left and you go under one of the old railway tunnels that carries a road over your head. Continue walking on the track next to the

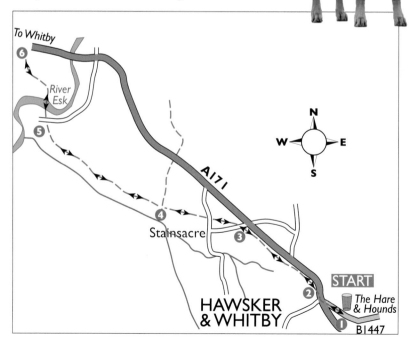

houses of Stainsacre and then out into the countryside once more as you leave the village behind you.

4 You now begin to walk on a wooded part of the Cinder Track, with trees on either side of the immediate path. It's a simple route to follow at this time and you should stick to the track as it veers slightly to the left and right.

5 A more pronounced curve around to the right brings you to one of the most notable features of the walk – the viaduct that takes the track over the River Esk. This huge structure designed to carry the railway towards Whitby has stood the test of time, still looking magnificent. Make time to peer over the wall at the amazing views you get from here. At the other side of the viaduct, the track bends round to the left and passes through more woodland before curving to the right and passing beneath another road.

6 The end of the Cinder Track brings you out at several industrial units. If you're wanting to head into Whitby to make your walk longer than the planned 6 miles, you should turn right onto the small road at this point, head through the small tunnel and proceed down the hill, following signs for Whitby town centre. If you've decided to head back and tuck into a pub lunch at the Hare and Hounds, it's simply a case of retracing your steps on the Cinder Track back to Hawsker and turning right onto the A171.

4 GOATHLAND
3 miles (4.8 km)

Ever since Nick Berry donned his 1960s police uniform and took the lead role in *Heartbeat*, Goathland has enjoyed celebrity status as the central location of the popular series. The village provided the setting for Aidensfield, having its buildings transformed back in time whenever filming took place. Fans of the show will be able to recognise many of the places in and around Goathland, including the train station, pub, shops and garage. There's plenty for people to look at around the village and on summer days it's likely to be fairly busy as the trains from the North York Moors Railway pull in. The walk itself is a suitable reflection of the glorious surroundings the village enjoys. You'll be taken to two stunning natural features – Beck Hole and Mallyan Spout – and there are spots by the river and near woods your dog will love. Do keep them under control near the river after heavy rain, though – West Beck can be fast flowing and potentially dangerous.

Start & Finish: Beck Hole Road, Goathland.
Sat Nav: YO22 5LZ.
Parking: Goathland Car Park on Beck Hole Road in the centre of the village.
OS Map: OS Explorer OL27 North York Moors Eastern Area.
Grid ref: NZ833013.

THE PUB Whether you know it as **THE GOATHLAND HOTEL** or the Aidensfield Arms, there's no mistaking this popular building which has featured in many of the *Heartbeat* episodes. Few pubs have such a strong link with popular TV shows and characters as this. Even though the show was cancelled years ago, fans of the 18 series that were made still flock to enjoy a pint at the pub. Dogs are allowed in all the public rooms of the hotel, allowing you to soak up the surroundings and order something to refresh yourself at the end of your walk. For those who weren't into *Heartbeat*, you'll find the unique features of this popular haunt, be it the tropical fish tank or the welcome given to families who are encouraged to play traditional games and read during their visit. To visit turn left out of the village car park and the hotel is on the right in 100 metres.

☎ 01947 896203   ⊕ thegoathlandhotel.co.uk

Terrain: Well established paths with some slopes.
Livestock: Sheep may be encountered on farming fields. Observe local signs.
Stiles: No stiles.
Nearest vet: Clevedale Vets, The Parade, Whitby, YO21 3JP.
☎ 01947 825042   ⊕ clevedalevets.co.uk

The Walk

. . . .

1 Having arrived in the village by either car or train, the walk starts by heading out of Goathland along the main road. You should start off turning right out of the car park or walking away from the railway station in the direction of Egton Bridge. Follow the road as it bends around to the left, heading for Mallyan Spout.

2 When you come to the church in ½ mile, take the path on the right-hand side of the road, heading through a gate. The path takes you by the side of a hotel, across a field and down the hill into a small wood.

3 At the bottom of the hill, there's a junction of paths and if you wish to go and see the wonderful Mallyan Spout you should head off to the left. Be careful on this section as it's rocky and slippery; make sure you are wearing sensible footwear. After viewing Mallyan Spout, return to the junction of paths and continue along the route you were initially taking,

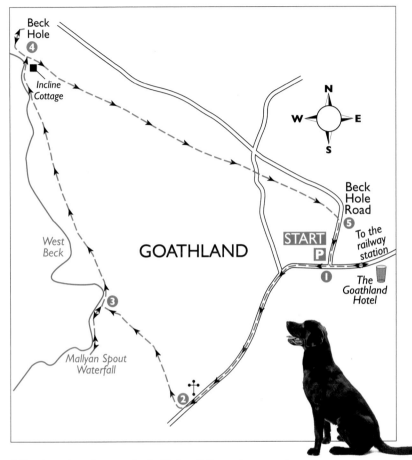

following the sign to Beck Hole. Follow the wooden
boardwalk through woodland and stick to the well-signed path as it climbs
over the fields.

4 When you reach the wonderfully named Incline Cottage in ¾ mile, there's
another junction of paths. Turn left and follow signs for Beck Hole to enjoy
another view of a natural feature. If you also head down to the road you will
reach the Birch Hall Inn, a charming and tiny pub famed for its Beck Hole
Butties. When you're finished, return to Incline Cottage and keep ahead to
follow the well-used path that leads back into Goathland.

5 The pathway back is easy to follow and takes you right back into Goathland,
crossing over a road on the way. In just over ¾ mile you'll arrive in the
village, where you turn right along the road to get back to the car park and
railway station.

5 GREAT AYTON & ROSEBERRY TOPPING
4 miles (6.1 km)

This stunning circular walk kicks off from the train station at Great Ayton, meaning that it's accessible for those wanting to arrive by rail as well as road. The popular dog friendly pub on this route is the King's Head Inn, which is reached via a short diversion just over halfway through the walk. Dogs will love this stroll because of the many woods there are to roam around, as well as the varied scents they'll be able to discover on the moorland. At the centre of the walk is the unmistakable summit of Roseberry Topping, an iconic pinnacle visible for miles around. It's one of the highest peaks in the North York Moors and the views you will get at the top are unforgettable. On a clear day you'll be able to gaze west and see the outline of the Pennines in the distance.

Start & Finish: Great Ayton station car park.
Sat Nav: TS9 6HQ .
Parking: At the station, or arrive on the train.
OS Map: OS Explorer OL26 North York Moors, Western Area.
Grid ref: NZ573108.

THE PUB

THE KING'S HEAD INN sits right at the foot of the wonderful Roseberry Topping in Newton under Roseberry, and is the perfect place to spend some time after the strenuous climb to the summit. It's a very popular place for dog walkers to head to and stay over, taking advantage of the many dog friendly paths that are in this area.

There's a warm welcome awaiting you at this pub, where dogs are allowed in the bar and they are also catered for in the rooms. You'll find yourself eating and drinking next to an eclectic bunch, with walkers, families and cyclists all enjoying the good hospitality in the fabulous countryside surroundings. Sat Nav: **TS9 6QR**.
☎ 01642 722318 ⊕ kingsheadinn.co.uk

> **Terrain:** Good footpaths, with some steep climbs and some great views to match them.
> **Livestock:** None. Observe local signs on the moors.
> **Stiles:** One stile.
> **Nearest vet:** Stokesley Veterinary Practice, 9 East End, Stokesley, TS9 5DP. ☎ 01642 710234 ⊕ stokesleyvets.co.uk

The Walk

• •

❶ Our walk sets off from the railway station, allowing people to arrive with their dogs on the train if they wish. After leaving the station, turn right along the road and head away from Great Ayton.

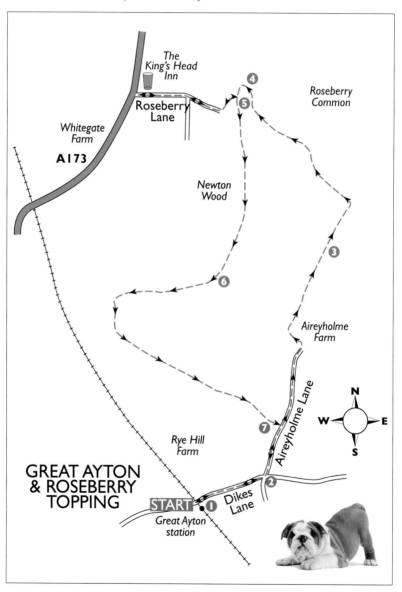

2 When you reach the junction of roads in 400 metres, turn left and head up Aireyholme Lane. This will take you winding up the hill, passing in and out of woodland in a section your dog will love exploring. When you reach a farm, walk to the other side of the yard and pick up the track again at the other side, turning right onto it and continuing to follow the signs up the hill for around ½ mile.

3 This track takes you further on up towards the summit, and it's very easy to follow. You'll eventually be brought to a drystone wall, where a gate gives access to the other side. Turn left onto this moorland path. This route will take you to the top of Roseberry Topping and for the final section there are stones that have been laid down to mark the way. Up it climbs to the summit, where you'll find a trig point and some of the best views in North Yorkshire. It's a steep final climb up, but well worth it.

4 Head down from the summit and continue in the same direction you had been heading in, aiming for Newton Wood at the far side of the folly. The path takes you to the right of the folly and then you follow it into the trees.

Pub Diversion: To reach the King's Head pub, turn right into the trees and follow the path through the wood. Turn left at the track you reach and then head down into the settlement where you'll find the King's Head. Retrace your footsteps to rejoin the walk.

5 If you are not heading to the pub, turn left here and follow the route that skirts along the edge of the wood. The trees open up at a clearing and there's a fork in the path where you need to keep left. This area is popular in the spring as the bluebells flower.

6 When you get to a T-junction of paths, turn right and head down the hill. This will take you out of the wood and to a wide track, where you should turn left. Soon after, there's a fork in the path and you should take the option on the left. This takes you into Cliff Ridge Wood, a nice plantation with plenty for your dog to explore. The path is simple to follow and at the far side of the wood it brings you out at a kissing gate.

7 At the other side of the gate, turn right on the path and follow it as it heads down to the road. There's a stile to cross over before you reach the road. Turn right and you'll be heading back to the train station.

6 RICCALL
Up to 13 miles (20.4 km)

South of York and north of Selby, the small village of Riccall is missed by most as they skirt alongside it on the A19. But this charming little North Yorkshire settlement has a very surprising claim to fame in that it sits right on the edge of our solar system. This relates to a wonderfully informative scale model of the solar system that has been placed along the former railway track running from Riccall to York. From tiny Pluto, you pass Uranus, Jupiter, Mars and the rest of the planets on the way to getting towards the huge Sun that sits some six and a half miles away. This is not just a great walk with a whole load of off-lead time, this is also a day out that will teach you plenty about our planet and outer space. Whether you're looking for a long or short walk from Riccall, this there-and-back route is ideal.

Start & Finish: Silver Street, Riccall. **Sat Nav: YO19 6TE**.
Parking: Street parking on Silver Street in the centre of Riccall.
OS Map: OS Explorer 290 York. **Grid ref:** SE620379.

THE PUB | **THE HARE & HOUNDS** is a traditional pub situated in the heart of the village. You can expect both you and your pooch to get a warm welcome when you go through the door after a day exploring the solar system. Whether you are looking for a hearty meal or a pint of fine ale, you'll have plenty of choice here.

☎ 01757 248255 ⊕ facebook.com/TheHareHounds8

Terrain: A well-used trail along the former East Coast Railway line. Some roadside walking.
Livestock: None.
Stiles: No stiles.
Nearest vet: Tower Veterinary Group, 170 Fulford Road, York, YO10 4DA. ☎ 01904 653961 ⊕ towervets.co.uk

The Walk

❶ With your back to the Hare and Hounds pub, turn left and when you reach Main Street turn left again. Keep ahead as the road turns into York Road.

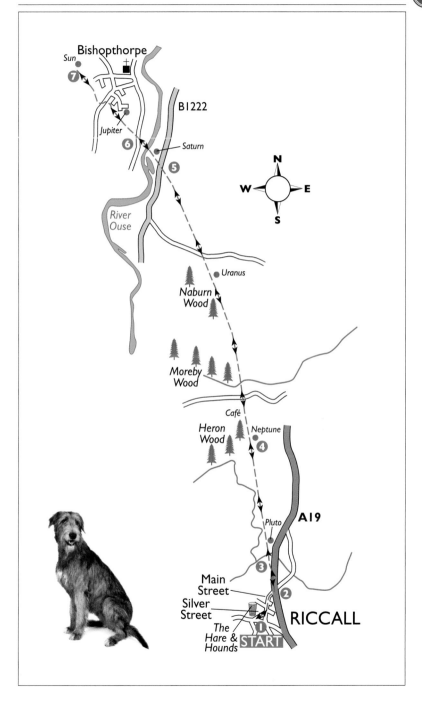

Bishopthorpe

Sun

7

B1222

Jupiter

6

Saturn

5

River Ouse

N
W **E**
S

Uranus

Naburn Wood

Moreby Wood

Café

Heron Wood

Neptune

4

A19

Pluto

3

Main Street

Silver Street

The Hare & Hounds

START

2

RICCALL

2 When you're brought out at the A19, turn left and stick to the walkway at the side of the road. After around 100 metres there is a turning to the left you need to take and this brings you to the start of the solar system trail. Look out for Pluto, up a track to the right.

3 Beyond Pluto, you get to fully appreciate how this used to be a railway line – the route is straight for a lengthy section and also on the level. The immediate route is tree lined with lots of scope for your dog to explore the long grasses and trees. Stick to the straight track and you'll soon come to Neptune.

4 The Neptune marker sits at the start of a small wood, and when you walk beyond it you will venture into the trees. The track is still straight and easy to follow, taking you beneath two bridges carrying roads above your head. Just after a slight bend to the left you'll come to Uranus. Press on ahead and the track continues its bend around to the left, passing a campsite and a conveniently placed café.

5 The walking trail passes over the B1222 and you should look out for the Saturn marker immediately after. The route is now about to go by the River Ouse and the first sign of this is the lovely marina you can see through the trees on the left.

6 What happens next on the walk is quite remarkable, not only because of the change in landscape as you enter the more urban setting of Bishopthorpe but also because you learn more about the structure of the solar system. After passing Jupiter, the route creeps nearer to houses and arrives at Appleton Close, where you should follow the bike trail signs. Turn left at the junction and then immediately right to pick up the path again. You then come across Mars, Earth, the moon,  Venus, Mercury and the massive Sun in quick succession, letting you know how relatively packed this corner of the solar system is.

7 If you've made it all the way to the Sun, this is the point where you turn around and retrace your steps back to Pluto and Riccall. You can, of course, make the decision to make the route shorter if you wish. The route back to the outer edge of the solar system is very straight forward and the trail is well signed all the way back to the A19. At that road, turn right and walk down York Road and then turn right at Silver Street to return to your car and the pub.

7 AUSTWICK
6 miles (10.1 km)

The local limestone is the star of the show on this beautiful circular walk from the picturesque Dales village of Austwick. As well as having a brilliant pub to relax in at the end, there's also a great tearoom halfway round and it's all in the setting of drystone walls and wonderful limestone outcrops high on the hills. Keep an eye out for Robin Proctor's Scar on the hill above Austwick – sitting on top of this are some sandstone erratics that were brought here by a glacier in the last Ice Age. Enjoy the freedom of strolling along country tracks next to the iconic limestone walls, giving your dog some rocky off-lead time.

Start & Finish: The Game Cock, High Street.
Sat Nav: LA2 8BB.
Parking: There is plenty of roadside parking on Main Street in the middle of Austwick near the pub.
OS Map: OL Explorer 2 Yorkshire Dales Southern & Western Areas.
Grid ref: SD767685.

THE PUB Dogs are extremely welcome in the bar of the **GAME COCK**, a traditional country inn located at the heart of Austwick. Thousands of walkers have taken their boots into this pub at the end of a trek onto the Yorkshire Dales hills, and you can see why it's a popular spot. The restaurant serves up award-winning food and there is a good range of drinks on sale too. The pub interior is cosy and there's no better feeling than settling down with a drink in front of the fire after a pleasant hike around the local paths. The pub also offers rooms for those wanting to make a longer stay.

☎ 01524 251226 ⊕ gamecockinn.co.uk

Terrain: Well established farm tracks and paths.
Livestock: When in farmers' fields you will need to keep your dog under control. Follow local signs.
Stiles: No stiles.
Nearest vet: Dalehead Veterinary Group, Station Road, Settle, BD24 9AA. ☎ 01729 823538 ⊕ daleheadvetgroup.co.uk

The Walk

. . . .

1 You start in the centre of Austwick at the Game Cock pub, ideally placed for a relaxing meal and drink at the end of the walk. As you face the pub, turn to your right and walk ahead on the road, passing the school and turning left onto Townhead Lane. Continue straight as the paved country road becomes more gravelly and rocky as you leave the village behind you.

2 When you reach the crossway of paths in just under ½ mile, keep going ahead on the track that becomes Crummack Lane. It bends to the right and then to the left. You should keep on this track as it passes a farm track on the right and takes you deeper into the Dales. The hill up on the right is something that will gain your attention constantly on this section, dotted as it is with limestone.

3 You'll come to a junction of paths, where Crummack Lane takes a sharp turn to the left. At this point, take White Stone Lane that turns off to the right, following signs for Wharfe. Follow the stone track for around 500 metres and

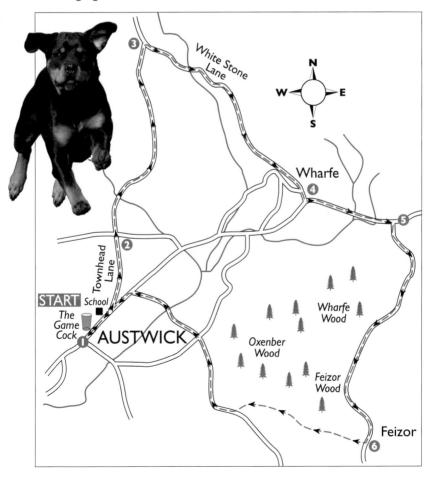

then take the bridge over Austwick Beck. White Stone Lane is easy to follow and in just under ¾ mile it will bring you into the centre of Wharfe.

4 From the middle of Wharfe, turn left along the track. It will lead you out of the hamlet, swinging to the right and soon after to the left before bringing you to a road. Go straight on along the road, which is also National Cycle Network

x

Route 68. Ignore the two tracks that lead off to buildings on the left, but then look out for the bridleway in just under ½ mile signed to the right.

5 This bridleway is signed for Feizor and is known as Bark House Lane. It twists and turns, heading through the buildings of Lower Bark House and pressing on towards Feizor. You climb a small hill as the bridleway rises up to Higher Bark House. Look out for the views of Ingleborough in the distance. You then begin a descent into Feizor, still sticking to the clear track.

6 Arriving in Feizor after ¾ mile, the walk passes the lovely tea rooms on the right, so feel free to pop in for some refreshment. Afterwards, keep going straight ahead as the route bends around to the right and in 100 metres take the track signed for Austwick to the right on Hale Lane. Continue along this track for 1½ miles, following signs for Austwick. It will take you over Austwick Beck once more and bring you out in the village. Turn left and you'll be heading for the pub!

8 THIRSK
3¾ miles (6 km)

A bustling market town in the heart of North Yorkshire, Thirsk is a great place to head for to base yourself for some superb walking. Although the population of the town is only around 5,000, Thirsk punches above its weight when it comes to facilities. This is down to the huge tourist appeal of the surrounding countryside, but also the literary significance of being the home of legendary vet James Herriot. After writing the classic books *If Only They Could Talk* and *It Shouldn't Happen to a Vet* among others, the rural tales of Herriot became known worldwide thanks to films and a long-running TV series. Thirsk is home to the World of James Herriot visitor attraction. This walk takes a circular route to nearby Sowerby, enjoying much of the countryside James Herriot loved.

Start & Finish: Marage Road, Thirsk. **Sat Nav: YO7 1AA** .
Parking: Marage Long Stay Car Park in the centre of Thirsk, on Marage Road.
OS Map: OS Explorer 302 Northallerton & Thirsk.
Grid ref: SE429823.

THE PUB **THE BLACK BULL** in the market square at the centre of Thirsk extends a warm welcome to dogs and their owners. This is clear from the sign outside the pub making you aware you can sit inside or out with your four-legged companion. It's conveniently located close to the start of the walk and also comes in handy if you need to do a spot of shopping while in the town centre. ☎ 01845 527188 ⊕ theblackbullthirsk.co.uk

Terrain: Easy going, well-trodden paths. Some roadside walking.
Livestock: None.
Stiles: No stiles.
Nearest vet: Skeldale Vets, York Road, Thirsk, YO7 3BT.
☎ 01845 522297 ⊕ skeldalevets.co.uk

The Walk

. . . .

1 From the car park, head back to Marage Road and turn left, heading towards St Mary's Church. Cross the road carefully and enter the church grounds, walking around the church on the left and then walking onto Cemetery Road. Turn right on Cemetery Road and follow this as it twists and turns through an 'S' bend.

2 Following Cemetery Road takes you out of built-up Thirsk and out into the farmland of Yorkshire. Soon you'll come to a T-junction, where you need to cross over Newsham Road and turn right. After around 50 metres, take the track on the left. As you walk down you'll be able to see a series of football pitches on the left and you'll also be walking around the back of Thirsk Racecourse. The lane you're on turns sharply to the left and then to the right before passing through a small wood. This stretch of the walk sees some amazing views opening up. On a clear day you'll be able to spot Ingleborough in the Yorkshire Dales.

3 Continue walking along this track, with good off-lead time, until the route diverts slightly to the right and then turns to the left. This section of the path runs parallel with the East Coast Mainline train route initially and then turns to get closer to it. Soon you'll find yourself following it and coming out at the Thirsk Station car park.

④ Leave the car park, turning left onto the road as you walk towards the Old Red House pub, which is another dog friendly pub you can enjoy a drink and snack in. From the pub car park, head through the kissing gate and enter the field, following the footpath signs that take you close to the railway track. Press onwards, crossing over the disused railway line that once went from Thirsk to Harrogate and then continue on through another field.

⑤ At the far side of this field, pass through another kissing gate and turn left onto Green Lane West. This is a very straight lane between farming fields, again another opportunity for off-lead time. In ¾ mile the farm track becomes a road and eventually enters a housing estate. Use the crossing to get to the other side of Topcliffe Road and then continue on along Green Lane East.

⑥ At Sowerby Road turn left, and cross over to reach the cycleway and footpath that crosses the field. Follow it towards the sports centre and turn right to go beyond the building. Turn left through the car park and after the first block of apartments turn right through a small passageway. You'll reach another car park here, where you should turn left and pass through it until you reach Nursery Gardens. Turn left on the road towards the A61, turning left again until you reach the main square. Turn right onto Millgate, where you will see the dog friendly Black Bull pub. Proceed down Millgate, soon turning left onto Marage Road and into the car park.

9 MASHAM
5 miles (7.5 km)

A beautiful **circular walk** from one of the most-loved towns in North Yorkshire, there'll be plenty of opportunity for you and your dog to have fun on this day out in Masham. The walking in this part of the world is great, with fields and rivers where you can stretch your legs. And it's fitting that this features in our dog walks from pubs guide because many regard this as the real ale capital of Northern England. For a relatively small town, it punches way above its weight when it comes to breweries. Masham boasts not one but two internationally known breweries. The oldest is the Theakston brewery, and Black Sheep was also established following a split in that famous brewing family. Needless to say, Masham is a beer-lovers' heaven as both breweries have several pubs in the area and visitor centres offering tours of the facilities. One word of warning, though! Don't come into town pronouncing the town's name as it appears when written. Masham is pronounced 'Mass-em' by locals, so now you know!

Start & Finish: Market Place, Masham. **Sat Nav: HG4 4DZ**.
Parking: There is plenty of parking in the main square at Masham, with an honesty box for motorists to contribute to.
OS Map: OS Explorer 298 Nidderdale.
Grid ref: SE225807.

THE PUB | **THE BRUCE ARMS** is a quality pub in the middle of Masham that's owned by the nearby Black Sheep Brewery. It's dog friendly and all canines are given a warm welcome, be it by the fire in the winter or in the rear beer garden during summer. It's this beer garden that provides the Bruce's main selling point as it's called 'the pub with the view' by those who come here often. The large space at the rear has a great panorama over Wensleydale and the River Ure, making it a spectacular place to sit when the sun is out. The wide range of ales and meals, along with the sign on the front welcoming dogs, make this the ideal place for a post-walk rest. You'll find the pub on Little Market Place, HG4 4DY, 100 metres from the main square. ☎ 01765 689372 ⊕ facebook.com/brucearmsmasham

Terrain: Well established paths, popular with dog walkers.
Livestock: Sheep may be encountered on the farming fields out of the town. Follow the advice of local signs.
Stiles: No stiles.
Nearest vet: Forrest House Vets, 5 Little Market Place, Masham, HG4 4DY. ☎ 01765 689219
⊕ forresthouse-veterinary.co.uk/our-practices/masham

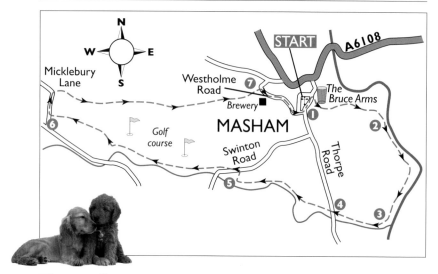

The Walk

1 This route starts in the town's main square. Apart from being easy to find, it's also a good place to base yourself and have a wander around the shops before you start. The pub that's linked to this walk is visible from the square, just down a side street. This makes it perfect for a pint before or after the walk. The church dominates the square and the walk starts by heading over to it and entering the churchyard. Walk down the side of the church and when you reach the other side you'll find the footpath you need to take, going through a gate. Turn left onto the track and move down the hill.

2 At the bottom, you will pass through another gate and need to turn right onto a track. Keep to the main track which takes you by the side of a house and you'll eventually come to the River Ure on your left and farming fields on the right. The path follows the course of the river as it steadily flows down this section, providing an attractive playground for dogs who love water.

3 Follow the path as it bends around to the right and starts to follow a small tributary that feeds into the River Ure. Take the path that leads down to the left and takes you closer to the water's edge. Continue to follow this smaller path as it sticks to the stream and climbs up the hill towards a road.

4 Cross over the road at Low Burn Bridge and pick up the path again on the other side, crossing over fields and following the easily spotted signs that mark out the route. The river stays on your left and the path moves away from it and then rejoins it, before leading the way across the fields towards another road (Swinton Road).

❺ Turn left onto the road and soon after follow the path leading off to the right. This takes you onto a golf course. If you head for the clubhouse you will see the signs indicating where the path veers off back to the river. The section of the walk that follows is a lovely stretch along the river, before eventually entering the golf course once more. Follow the signs that clearly tell you to follow a track away from the golf course and in around 1 mile you'll reach another road (Micklebury Lane).

❻ After turning right onto the road, head steadily up the hill. In 200 metres look out for the point where there's a track going straight ahead as the road bends to the left. Here, you should follow the path on the right that heads over fields. Very soon, the spire of Masham's church comes into view and you must now follow the signs across the fields to get back to the town centre.

❼ In ½ mile you'll reach a large animal feed works and should go beyond that, turning right onto Westholme Road. This will take you by the Theakston brewery. Follow the road around to the left as it passes the fire station. Turn left when you reach the junction and you'll be on course for heading back to the main square.

10 DRAX
5 miles (7.8 km)

What at first may not look like a typical spot for walking the dog is actually a very popular area, and there are very good reasons why. Beneath the huge cooling towers of Drax Power Station there are well-trodden paths that pass through some beautiful countryside, along with plenty of woodland for your dog to play in. The vantage points across the power station are fascinating and you're sure to be in good company with other dogs to meet. Known as the 'Energy Path,' this is one of the best kept secrets and a lovely walk in one of the quieter places of North Yorkshire.

Start & Finish: Drax Sports & Social Club.
Sat Nav: YO8 8PH .
Parking: Drax Sports & Social Club car park off the A645 near Drax.
OS Map: OS Explorer 291 Goole & Gilberdyke.
Grid ref: SE664263.

THE PUB

THE HUNTSMAN is a lovely, traditional pub in the heart of the village that prides itself on being dog friendly. Expect a warm welcome and to see plenty of locals with their canines in here as well. Enjoy a range of beers and some pub grub in this quiet village on the edge of North Yorkshire.

Check the website for up-to-date food serving times, and note that on Tuesdays the menu in the pub is replaced by a pizza van that serves in the car park. ☎ 01757 618642 ⊕ thehuntsmanindrax.co.uk

Terrain: Easy going, well-trodden paths.
Livestock: None.
Stiles: No stiles.
Nearest vet: Vets4Pets Selby, Bawtry Road, Selby, YO8 8LY.
☎ 01757 211610 ⊕ vets4pets.com

The Walk

. . . .

❶ Starting from the power station's sports and social club car park, head up the ramp to the road and turn left on the pavement. Cross over the railway bridge and then take the track left heading down through the trees. At the bottom, pick up the track right which will take you to the golf course. Turn right when you meet a larger track and carefully cross the road at the top.

❷ Go through the car park and pick up the track going into the woods. Head

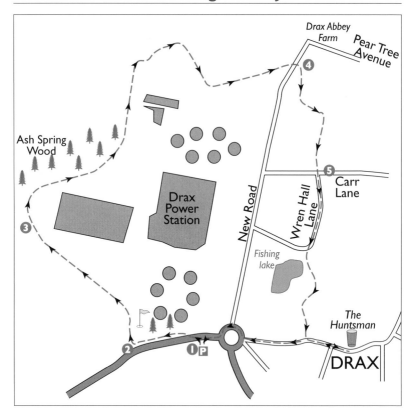

down some steps and follow the path, with the power station on the right. You'll eventually end up walking by the fence and views of the countryside open up when you clear the trees. This is the Energy Path and there are occasional information boards where you can read up about the business of electricity generation.

❸ In ¾ mile you'll reach the southern edge of Ash Spring Wood where there is a picnic bench and the path splits in two. Follow the route to the right which takes you amongst trees for over a mile. Occasionally, the well-signed path twists close to the power station and you go by the large fences. There is a lot of potential for off-lead time here and your dog will love investigating the smells of the woodland. More information boards tell you what happens at various stages of the process and there are a couple of really good vantage points to stop and have a nosy when you cross over footbridges.

4 You're brought out onto a road just south of Drax Abbey Farm; turn left here and go beyond a farm onto Pear Tree Avenue. After joining another path, take an immediate right turn onto a track running at the side of the field. Follow the pathway signs across the field and beneath the power lines for ½ mile until you're brought out at Carr Lane.

5 Cross over the road here and press on down Wren Hall Lane. When the road takes a sharp bend around to the right, continue on the path straight ahead. When the path splits at a fishing lake, take the route on the right that soon brings you out at Back Lane. You'll find yourself on the edge of Drax village. Turn left and walk into the village to reach the pub – you'll soon see it on the left. Alternatively, head right along the roadside paths to get back to the car park.

11 Tan Hill
8½ miles (13.9 km)

Make your way to one of the most remote spots in North Yorkshire to combine a walk on a famous path with a drink at a well-known pub. Britain's highest hostelry at 528 metres above sea level is the Tan Hill Inn, found in wild moorland surroundings on the Pennine Way. The 'middle of nowhere' location of this fabulous walk is one of the biggest appeals. The weather can be blustery and harsh, but plan this route on a glorious day and you'll be in your element. There's a real 'top of the world' feeling at Tan Hill, and it's rare that you can find yourself away from it all with such a good watering hole to welcome muddy boots and paws at the end of it.

Start & Finish: Tan Hill Inn, Long Causeway.
Sat Nav: DL11 6ED.
Parking: There is plenty of parking at the pub and along the roadside opposite.
OS Map: OL Explorer 19 Howgill Fells & Upper Eden Valley.
Grid ref: NY897066.

NORTH YORKSHIRE – Dog Friendly Pub Walks

THE PUB To say the **TAN HILL INN** is dog friendly is a bit of an understatement. When we called in after the walk, there were many happy pooches in the bar and they get just as warm a greeting as the humans. Many of the dog owners come back time and again because of the friendliness towards dogs, who are welcome in the bar area and can stay over in the rooms as well. It's even known for the pub to put on events for dog owners, such as a dog friendly firework display to mark Bonfire Night. The establishment has a history that dates back to the coaching inn days of the 17th century, and has the welcoming features of

Photo by Sylvia Raw

stone floors, an open fire and exposed beams that you might expect. The surroundings are just as exquisite. This is a corner of England that has seen much change over the centuries and it's a joy to spend time there.

☎ 01833 533007 ⊕ tanhillinn.com

Terrain: Well established paths, popular with dog walkers. A short section is on a country road.

Livestock: Sheep and birds may be encountered on some aspects of the walk. Observe local signage and ensure your dog is well behaved.

Stiles: No stiles.

Nearest vet: Forrest House Vets, 5 Little Market Place, Masham, HG4 4DY. ☎ 01765 689219

⊕ forresthouse-veterinary.co.uk/our-practices/masham

The Walk

. . . .

1 As you face the inn, head off to the right and take the footpath on the

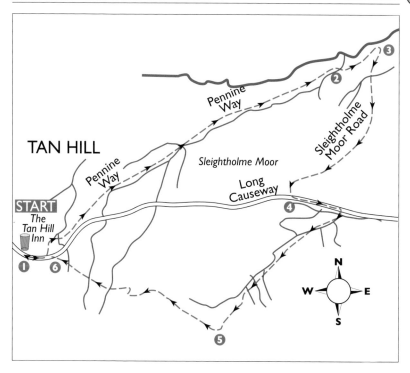

left that sets off across Sleightholme Moor. This is a well established path that is easy to follow and well laid out with marks because it is the route of the Pennine Way. The path takes you across a couple of small streams and then bends round to the right and runs parallel to Coal Gill Syke.

2 Continue to follow the Pennine Way across the moor, taking in the superb 360 degree views that you are afforded in this part of the world. The larger hills will be behind you, so keep having a check back to look out for Great Shunner Fell. In 3¼ miles you come to a more substantial track, where you turn right.

3 In 1¼ miles, and after passing a series of shooting butts on your right, you'll be brought to a T-junction where you need to turn right. This is Sleightholme Moor Road, a substantial track that takes you through the often boggy moor. You're now on the W2W cycle route, which runs from Walney to Weir, one of several cross-country biking journeys that dissect North Yorkshire.

4 Turn left onto the road (Long Causeway) and follow the country route for about ¾ mile before taking the footpath signed off to the right. This will take you across the moorland once again, pretty much following the small stream known as William Gill.

5 In 1½ miles you'll reach a footpath signed off to the right and should take this, passing through a country once busy with small coal pits – some of which you can still see evidence of. Stick to the path to remain safe as some of the shafts in the area are uncovered. Make sure your dog is on a lead here.

6 On reaching the road, turn right to wind up back at the pub.

12 LEYBURN
6 miles (9.5 km)

Combining the delights of the North Yorkshire countryside with the charms of a beautiful market town, there is a choice of dog friendly pubs to indulge in after the walk is finished. Leyburn is also proud of its participation in sporting events. There was a big crowd in the town to see the Olympic torch pass through in 2012 and two years later there was a great turnout to welcome the cyclists in the Tour de France, with the Tour de Yorkshire passing through in 2018. You may well see a few proudly exhibited yellow bicycles around the town to mark the occasion. In fact, across North Yorkshire you're likely to come across quite a few yellow bicycles in the various villages this book visits. This is a legacy of the 2014 Tour De France, which had the first two days held in Yorkshire and saw the peloton race through during Stage 1. Ever since the Yorkshire crowds welcomed the cyclists so warmly and held parties in the streets, the Tour de Yorkshire has become an annual event and Leyburn has also featured in this. Halfway around this walk, there's a small country tearoom called the Yorkshire Tea Party that you might want to enjoy a cuppa at. If you do, you'll be in good company. This part of the Dales has a Victorian history of putting on jolly good tea parties, and they still do it really well in the converted 1960s caravan you'll be walking past. Leyburn's tea party heritage started back in 1841 when the town's tradesmen started laying out the Shawl and putting seats in for visitors to enjoy the views. To celebrate the opening, on July 31st, they held a tea party on the Shawl and it was so popular that it became an annual event. There were bands who came to perform and the event was generally attended by thousands of people who came from all over the region to enjoy the views, nice food and a good cup of tea. The last of these great Victorian events was held in 1858, but at the foot of the Shawl there's still a good cuppa to be had, as well as the selection of tearooms in the town that are awaiting your tired legs at the end of the walk.

Start & Finish: Market Place, Leyburn. **Sat Nav: DL8 5AP**.
Parking: Pay and display car park on Market Place in the centre of Leyburn.
OS Map: OS Explorer 30 Yorkshire Dales Northern & Central Areas. **Grid ref:** SE112905.

THE PUB — **THE GOLDEN LION**, one of the most prominent buildings in Leyburn's much-loved market square, is a Grade II listed building and dates back to the 1850s. Today, this family-run pub is somewhere you are sure to get a warm Yorkshire welcome – and a tasty meal with a thirst-quenching pint. The pub is openly dog friendly, with your

pet being allowed into the bar and also in the 14 bedrooms if you decide you'd like to stay over and indulge in a hearty full English breakfast. ☎ 01969 622161 ⊕ goldenlionleyburn.co.uk

> **Terrain:** Well established paths that climb gentle slopes. Small amount of road walking.
> **Livestock:** Sheep may be encountered on farming fields. Observe local signs.
> **Stiles:** Two stiles.
> **Nearest vet:** Yoredale Vets, Leyburn Business Park, Harmby Road, Leyburn, DL8 5QA. ☎ 01969 623024 ⊕ yoredalevets.co.uk

The Walk

1 From the main square, head down the hill, along the A684 towards the train station. When you reach the crossroads with the petrol station, make sure you're on the right-hand side of the road. Turn right here and take the path that doubles back on your route. You'll see the train track down on your right for 100 metres before you take the left fork. Follow the path ahead as it bends to the left.

2 Carry on down the hill and you'll come to a quiet road (Park View), where you'll see the continuation of the path on the other side and slightly to the right. Carry on along this and you'll be brought out into fields. Head straight

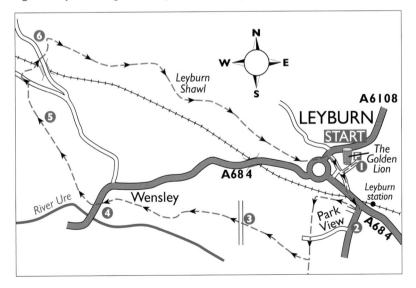

down the grass field and pass through a gap in the wall but before you get to the end of the large field, there is a path to take on your right; be careful to find this because it's not marked with a signpost, but there will be a gap in the wall over on the right where the path leaves the field. Follow this path across the fields, passing through gates and eventually reaching a lane where a stream sometimes runs down after wet weather.

❸ On reaching this lane, head up the other side and continue on the path through the fields. From field to field, follow the path as it takes you towards a nature reserve in ½ mile and eventually brings you close to the River Ure, which flows on your left. There are a couple of stiles on this section of the walk. If you stick with the wall on your left and follow the path, in just over another ½ mile you'll reach the village of Wensley, which is of course the place that lends its name to this most famous of dales.

❹ At Wensley, when you reach the track turn left onto it and follow it until you get to the road, where you turn right and go past the church on your left. At the main road, turn right and then immediately take the track on the left that goes through the impressive gates. You're now at the main entrance to Bolton Hall, but you're not going all the way to the house. Instead, look out for the path that turns off on the right and heads up a grassy hill. This track will take you past a few isolated trees as you head towards a wood and go by a farm building on the left.

❺ Stick to the path after this steep climb up the grassy hill. Go through a gate and cross another field towards the trees. A track through the wood will bring you out at a road where you need to turn left and then keep an eye out for a footpath turning off to the right in 200 metres. When you take this, you'll head across a field and over the train track – take care here as trains do use it regularly. Walk over the next field, which can get very muddy, and then go across the road and over Keld Bridge, following the path round to the right as it passes the café and bends to the left going up the hill.

❻ When you've gone beyond the farm, take the path on the right that takes you onto a track and when you have a choice of paths you should choose the one on the right that goes straight on. This section is easy to follow, passing through fields and then branching to the left in ½ mile up towards the top of a ridge known as Leyburn Shawl. Turn right onto this larger track and enjoy the views out over Wensleydale on the right and the modern edge given to the quarry on the right which is now adorned in solar panels. You just need to stick to this well-defined track for 1 mile as it brings you back into Leyburn, passing a park on your left as you do so. You'll come to a road, which you follow to reach the main square once more when you reach the end of it.

13 BOLTON ABBEY
6 miles (9.9 km)

The magnificent ruined abbey is one of the first things you'll see on this magnificent circular walk at the southern end of the Yorkshire Dales, easily accessible and close to good roads. Information boards and extremely atmospheric surroundings allow you to get immersed in local history, while the real adventure for your dog starts a little further on. There are off-lead opportunities next to the river and through the woods on an extremely varied walk with plenty of fabulous scenery to take in. Factor in a lovely country hotel to get a pint, as well as a brilliant café along the way, and you have the ingredients for a quality day out at any time of the year.

Start & Finish: Bolton Abbey Car Park. **Sat Nav: BD23 6EX**.
Parking: There is pay and display parking at the abbey car park, well signposted on your way into Bolton Abbey.
OS Map: OS Explorer 2 Yorkshire Dales Southern & Western Areas.
Grid ref: SE070538.

THE PUB | **THE DEVONSHIRE ARMS** cannot be missed on the road to Bolton Abbey and is not far from the start point for the walk, giving you the option of popping in either before or after the amazing stroll by the river. You're sure of a warm welcome for your dog, whether you go in for a drink or decide to stay overnight at this charming hotel. There are spare bowls, leads, waste bags and even washing areas on hand for your dog. You are welcome to take your dog into the hotel lounges for afternoon tea, drinks or a lunch between 1.30pm and 4.30pm as well. Although they're not allowed in the restaurant, well-behaved dogs can stay at the reception. The location, less than ½ mile along the B6160 from Bolton Abbey, is stunning and as well as this walk there are plenty of other off-road routes to explore.
☎ 01756 718100 ⊕ thedevonshirearms.co.uk

Terrain: Well established paths, with moderately steep climbs in the woods along the riverside route. Some rocky areas can be slippery.
Livestock: Sheep may be encountered on the fields near the abbey.
Stiles: No stiles.
Nearest vet: Ashlands Veterinary Centre, 119 Leeds Road, Ilkley, LS29 8JS. ☎ 01943 817000 ⊕ ashlandsvets.co.uk

The Walk

. . . .

1 From the car park, head beyond the toilet block to the main road into the village and turn left. Look out for the gap in the wall on the right and go through it. Go through the gate into the field at the other side and follow the path down to the footbridge going over the river.

2 Cross the river, either using the footbridge or the stepping-stones if you're feeling a little more adventurous. Be careful though because after heavy rain the stones can be difficult to pass over. At the other side, turn left and start to walk on the riverside path. There's plenty here for dogs to explore and they'll be in their element on this easy going path next to the water.

3 You'll be brought out at a road and should turn left onto it, crossing over the ford and taking the path on the left once more. This heads into more woodland, with the river on the left again.

Barden
Bridge **5**

P

P

N
W **E**
S

4 Posforth
Bridge

B6160

6
Café

3

River
Wharfe

The
Devonshire
Arms

BOLTON ABBEY

2

1 ■
P
START

4 After following the path next to the river for ½ mile you will be brought out at another road at Posforth Bridge. Turn left here and follow the riverside route once more, heading in the direction of Barden Bridge. This will take you through a nice conservation area and there is a bit of an incline to deal with in this section, but you're rewarded by the view from the top, where you'll also find a bench and a shelter. This section of the walk is fairly high above the river and you'll be able to look down on waterfalls and a gorge – known as the Strid. Once you cross over a small stream you'll have picturesque Barden Bridge in your view.

5 Cross over the bridge and pick up the path on the other side, heading to the left and this time following the river as it heads downstream. After around ½ mile there is a wooden bridge to cross and then you should stick to the path for a further 1¼ miles as it follows the course of the river and returns to Bolton Abbey. There are many fabulous features to see on this stretch of the Strid as the waterfalls and rock formations come thick and fast.

6 When you reach the café, cross over the river using the footbridge and pick up the path on the other side, retracing your steps back down to the abbey. Follow the Dales Way, cross the ford and pick up the path on the right. You'll be brought out once again at the bridge near the abbey. Cross over here and head up the hill to the gap in the wall, near the car park.

14 MALHAM
4 miles (6.2 km)

One of the many jewels in the Yorkshire Dales, Malham is a hugely popular place to go walking with or without a dog. There are so many incredible features here to stroll around, from the impressive Malham Cove to gorges, waterfalls and the awe-inspiring limestone pavement. The superb limestone scenery means you'll be reaching for your camera at every turn. There are rivers and woods for your dog to explore, while you need to pay attention to local signs and ensure you use a lead when required. Part of the area's attraction is that it's farming country, which means there may well be sheep about. Harry Potter fans are in for a treat when they reach the limestone pavement; this is the place where the fictional wizard camped in the film version of *The Deathly Hallows*.

Start & Finish: Malham Car Park. **Sat Nav: BD23 4DJ**.
Parking: There is pay and display parking at the car park near the visitor centre in Malham, and some roadside parking before you get to the village.
OS Map: OS Explorer 2 Yorkshire Dales Southern & Western Areas.
Grid ref: SD899627.

NORTH YORKSHIRE – Dog Friendly Pub Walks

THE PUB Situated in the heart of the village, **THE BUCK INN** offers everything dogs and their owners require after an invigorating walk in the Yorkshire Dales. The welcoming sign outside sums it up perfectly – dogs and muddy boots are welcome here! Bliss! It's a traditional country pub with a good range of ales and good bar menu. The biggest thing the pub has going for it is the location. As soon as you step out of the door you are in the heart of some fantastic limestone scenery and only a short stroll from beautiful Malham Cove. You'll find the Buck on Cove Road, BD23 4DA, 200 metres from the visitor centre car park. ☎ 01729 830317 ⊕ thebuckmalham.co.uk

Terrain: Well established paths, with a steep climb up steps from Malham Cove. Extreme care is needed walking along the limestone pavement.
Livestock: Depending on the time of year, you may come across some. Observe local signs and be sensible.
Stiles: No stiles.
Nearest vet: Dalehead Veterinary Group, Station Road, Settle, BD24 9AA. ☎ 01729 823538 ⊕ daleheadvetgroup.co.uk

The Walk

● ●

① We set out from the main car park in Malham. A visitor centre is also here and worth popping in for a look. Walk on the roadside from here into the centre of Malham. Look out for the traditional smithy on the right, still producing a range of Yorkshire Dales produce such as fire pokers with a sheep design. Continue through Malham and you'll see the dog friendly pub, the Buck Inn, on the left. The walk continues beyond the pub for just over ¼ mile, sticking to the road and following signs for Malham Cove.

② Take the path on the right heading for Malham Cove. Initially, this is a fenced-in path just to get you off the road, but it soon opens out into countryside and you then follow it across paths towards Malham Cove, which you can see in the distance. There's the opportunity for your dog to explore the river which runs out from beneath the cove. The wall of the cove itself is awe-inspiring, and there are often people trying to climb up its face.

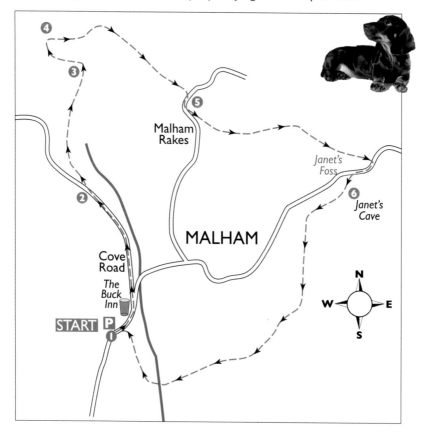

3 Turn left and follow the path up the most challenging section of the walk. There's a series of steep steps to negotiate as you gain height quickly. Of course, although the climb is tough there is also a big reward coming your way in terms of the view behind you, which becomes more and more extensive as you head on up. At the top you're faced with one of the best limestone pavements in the Yorkshire Dales. It's stunning scenery, like a lunar landscape, though you must take care when walking across the potentially slippery limestone.

4 Head across the limestone pavement towards a drystone wall and a junction of paths. Go straight on and stick to this path as it starts to climb Sheriff Hill, although it soon starts to descend all the way down the grassy hill to a road (Malham Rakes).

5 Turn right onto the road, but then take the path on the other side soon after. There is now an easy to follow path that guides you across a series of farming fields and brings you to another country road (Gordale Lane). Turn right onto the road and in about 100 metres take the path on the left. You'll now be walking by the side of Gordale Beck, and very soon you'll come to the crashing waterfall, Janet's Foss.

6 Continue straight ahead on what is an obvious path to stick to. You'll be brought to a footbridge and soon after a junction of different paths. Turn right and follow the path by the side of Malham Beck. When you reach another footbridge, cross it to reach the main road in Malham again and turn left to return to the car park.

15 GARGRAVE
6½ miles (10.3 km)

Often overlooked in favour of nearby Skipton or Settle, Gargrave has plenty to offer walkers looking for a great day out. Two key routes pass through here, the most famous being the long-distance Pennine Way that winds a steady way over the hills towards Scotland. But we're focussing on the fabulous towpath at the side of the Leeds-Liverpool Canal. It provides an often-underestimated resource for dog walkers, and one that you'll want to return to after discovering it. There's a lot of off-lead time here and the beauty is you can keep on going for a longer walk if you wish!

Start & Finish: North Street, Gargrave. **Sat Nav: BD23 3RN**.
Parking: The North Street Car Park in the centre of Gargrave.
OS Map: OS Explorer 2 Yorkshire Dales Southern & Western Areas.
Grid ref: SD933543.

THE PUB

THE MASONS ARMS has a brilliant location on the Pennine Way and is close to the Leeds-Liverpool Canal, making it an ideal stop off for those who find their adventures bringing them to Gargrave. It markets itself as a good Yorkshire pub and has a wide range of food, sourced with local ingredients, and drink on offer – as well as accommodation for those wanting to stay over. Dogs are welcome throughout, including with those booking rooms. ☎ 01756 749304 ⊕ masonsarmsgargrave.co.uk

Terrain: Easy going, well-trodden paths.
Livestock: Likely to be some on the final stages.
Stiles and roads: Some stiles on the farmland entering Gargrave.
Nearest vet: Ashlands Veterinary Centre, Rockvilla, 1-3 Clifford Street, Skipton, BD23 2AD. ☎ 01756 636999 ⊕ www.ashlandsvets.co.uk

The Walk

❶ Turn right out of the car park to walk along North Street away from the main road until you get to a junction. Turn right along West Street, following the sign for the Leeds–Liverpool Canal. This becomes Mark House Lane and will take you to the canal itself in 100 metres.

❷ When you arrive at the canal, turn left and follow the towpath in the direction of Liverpool – don't worry, you're not going that far! This is a long, flat path and it's all fantastic for off-lead time. With the water and other dogs you'll meet, there's sure to be a great time had by all on this stretch of the walk.

❸ The path continues on under the railway bridge and over the river following the route of the canal until it brings you out at a road. Turn right here onto the road and follow it round to the left for 200 metres until it brings you out to the canal path once more. You'll now be walking in the same direction as before but on the other side of the canal.

❹ In ¼ mile you'll come to a series of locks at Bank Newton. Keep going, past the Mike Clarke lock, and continue walking on the canal towpath. Carry on for 2 miles, passing the Langber TV station. Soon after this, take the left-hand track you find at the bridge and continue along it. (Here is a good point to retrace your steps back along the canal to Gargrave if stiles and the possibility of encountering livestock is a problem.)

❺ After around 200 metres, look out for the Pennine Way sign on the left and the take this well-known route as it doubles back on the path. The route takes you across a field, by a wood and then crosses another field before coming to a lane. After a short section on a rural track, take the Pennine Way once again off to the right.

❻ This section of the walk is easy to follow, taking you across farming fields into Gargrave. It's very well sign-posted and takes you to the right of Scaleber Hill. When you reach a crossroads of paths after 1 mile, continue straight ahead along the Pennine Way again.

❼ After crossing over the railway via a bridge, take the path on the right and cross the last few fields before being brought out at a road (Church Street). Turn left onto it and head back to the centre of Gargrave. You'll see the Masons Arms on the left so you can relax at the end of your walk.

16 KELD

6 miles (9.7 km)

A beautiful walk in the heart of the Yorkshire Dales, there is plenty for you and your dog to enjoy on this circular stroll from Keld. The pub is located on the main road and is a great place to warm up and relax after walking through fields, taking in the magnificent waterfalls and enjoying the stunning views. This is in the middle of limestone country and has more than its fair share of superb drystone walls and beautiful rivers. There are spots where your dog will be able to go in for a splash in the River Swale, which has carved out the incredible Swaledale over the centuries. Nearby, the town of Hawes has shops and more dog friendly pubs. You may want to stay over here and take advantage of the dog walk from Hawes also featured in this book.

Start & Finish: The car park in Keld that is near the farm and campsite. **Sat Nav: DL11 6LJ** .
Parking: From the main road, head down into Keld and you'll find parking next to a farm with an honesty box.
OS Map: OL Explorer 30: Yorkshire Dales Northern & Central Areas.
Grid ref: NY892012.

THE PUB Sitting on the road that connects Keld to Hawes (B6270), **KELD LODGE** is a building that dominates the surrounding area and commands good views over Swaledale. It was originally built as a shooting lodge in 1860 but has served ramblers as a hotel and restaurant since 2007. The lodge owners pride themselves as being pet friendly, and this is flagged up in signs at the bar and information on the website. Dogs – as well as your muddy boots – are welcome throughout the lodge, apart from in the dining room. Enjoy a good range of great food and ales at Keld Lodge, and make sure you

chat to some of the other people who are calling in. Because it's located close to the Pennine Way, the Coast to Coast trail and the Herriot Way, expect to see long-distance walkers who have come here from all over the planet.
☎ 01748 886259 ⊕ keldlodge.com

Terrain: Well established paths, popular with dog walkers. Potentially boggy in some places after rain. Some steep sections.
Livestock: Sheep may be encountered on the farming fields out of the town. Follow the advice of local signs.
Stiles: No stiles.
Nearest vet: Pendragon Vets, Kirkby Stephen, CA17 4HT.
☎ 017683 71359 ⊕ pendragonvets.co.uk

The Walk

❶ From the car park in Keld that is near the farm and campsite, head back to the road and follow the bridleway down the hill, signed as the Coast to Coast walk. When you get down to the bottom of the hill, turn left and pick up the Pennine Way. Take the bridge across the river and you'll see a lovely waterfall on your right – East Gill Force.

❷ On the other side of the river, go straight ahead and turn left onto the Pennine Way. A steep climb will bring you up to a house. Turn left here and make your way along the public bridleway. There are such great views to enjoy here down to the valley bottom on the left. The route continues ahead for ½ mile and then goes down into a dip, passing the lovely Currack Force and climbing up the slope on the other side of it.

3 Climb the small hill and when you reach the top there is a gate to go through and a road (Stonesdale Lane) to cross. The path continues at the other side for ½ mile. As the path crosses over fields, the view down to the valley includes another waterfall – Wain Wath Force. Take care when the path goes near the steep drop to the left. After walking through some wooded areas, where your dog may love the chance to explore different scents, the route heads uphill again and brings you to a track. Turn right onto it and continue climbing, passing a number of ruined buildings.

4 On your way up the hill you will come to a Coast to Coast footpath marker and it's here where you need to turn right and begin the return leg of the journey. The turn almost sees you heading back on yourself – look out for the abandoned buildings you've just gone by. This part of the walk can be tricky, but you'll be fine if you stick close to the wall on the right.

5 The path will bring you to the small village of West Stonesdale. As you enter the valley on the way into it, stick to the right and you'll be brought out at a road. Turn left onto the road and take the path on the right immediately after. Stick to the path, which is well signed, and then cross over the footbridge. At the far side of the bridge, turn left and follow the riverside path up the valley.

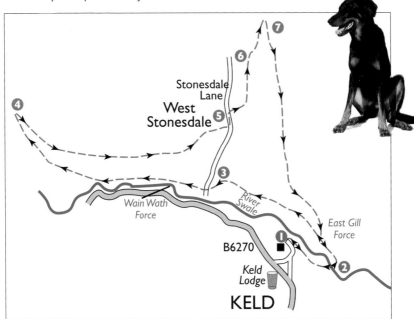

6 When you come to another footbridge crossing the river, take the path that bends off to the right towards a building. Climb up the hill, following the path and heading for the wall at the top. There's a stile at the top and on the other side of the wall you should take the path off to the left up the hill. Very quickly you'll come to a much larger track; this is the Pennine Way and you turn right here.

7 Follow the Pennine Way as it slowly descends. Go through the gates and follow the signs and this famous path will bring you back down to the waterfall you passed at the start of the walk. Cross over the footbridge and follow the path back up the hill to Keld to reach the starting point.

17 HAWES
3¾ miles (6.1 km)

There are a lot of reasons for making the trip to Hawes, from the fabulous walks to the breathtaking waterfalls and the chance to sample a fair helping of cheese. Plenty of dog friendly pubs await you in the town and you'll come across many dog owners who are up in North Yorkshire making a holiday of all the region has to offer. Hawes is in Wensleydale, which is of course the cheese capital of Yorkshire, and this is reflected in the chance to visit the creamery and the number of local hostelries that offer dishes featuring the local delicacy. The walk itself stretches your legs over the hills to Aysgill Force, a spectacular waterfall that rewards your climb.

Start & Finish: Market Place, Hawes. **Sat Nav: DL8 3QX** .
Parking: Pay and display car park on Market Place in the centre of Hawes.
OS Map: OS Explorer 30 Yorkshire Dales Northern & Central Areas.
Grid ref: SD872898.

THE PUB **THE BOARD INN**, right in the middle of Hawes, is a traditional Yorkshire pub ideally placed for exploring the Yorkshire Dales. Dogs are guaranteed a good welcome inside or outside whether you're drinking or eating and you'll see dog bowls put out for them to quench their thirst. Stay for food and you'll experience a hearty pub meal cooked from local ingredients wherever possible, cutting down on the food miles and boosting the local economy. If you fancy staying in Hawes for longer than a day, the Board Inn offers rooms and many of them are dog friendly.

☎ 01969 667223 ⊕ theboardinn.co.uk

Terrain: Well established paths that climb gentle slopes. Small amount of road walking.
Livestock: Sheep may be encountered on farming fields. Observe local signs.
Stiles: No stiles.
Nearest vet: Pendragon Vets, Kirkby Stephen, CA17 4HT.
☎ 017683 71359 ⊕ pendragonvets.co.uk

The Walk

. . . .

1 After parking up in the centre of Hawes, head for the main road and make your way towards the church. A path heading up the hill next to the church marks the starting point for your walk to discover some of the waterfalls of the Yorkshire Dales. The path is signed for Gayle and will lead you around the back of the church and then across a field, with the small Gayle Beck on the left. After going through a couple of gates the path brings you out at a road. Turn left here and walk into the small village of Gayle.

2 When you come to the junction in Gayle, turn right and continue to walk along the small country road until you leave the village. Carry on along here

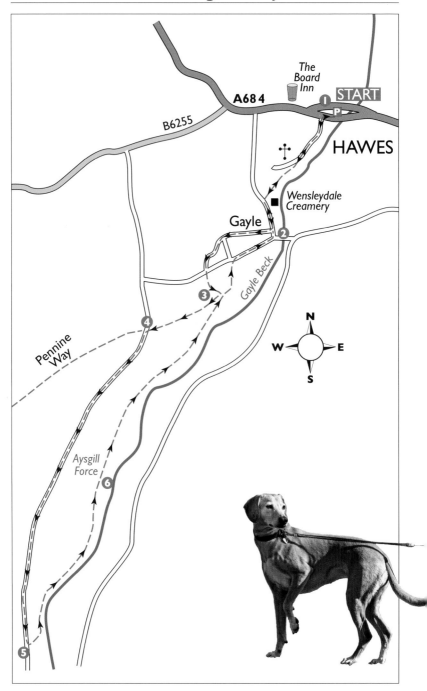

until you come to another junction, where you need to turn right and then take the path immediately on your left. The path presses on across a couple of fields, and it's an easy one to follow.

❸ Look out for the signpost marking out the route of the Pennine Way, then turn right along this historic long-distance footpath. As you'd expect, the Pennine Way is a well-marked footpath and is straight forward to follow across the series of fields that follows.

❹ You'll get brought out at a road and need to turn left onto it, continuing along this country road for a short distance until you see a track on the right. This is signed as Beggarman's Road and is one of the typically picturesque tracks in the Yorkshire Dales that has drystone walls made of limestone hemming you in, ideal for a bit of off-lead time. There are several gates to pass through as you make your way along this country lane, and all the time you are able to enjoy the stunning Yorkshire Dales scenery around you. You need to follow this track for just under a mile, taking the path through the metal gate on the left and following it downhill to the river.

❺ Just before you get to the river, follow the footpath sign sending you off to the left. The path you're now on goes through a gap in the limestone wall, past a ruined building and through another gate. Following the path on the left side of the river, head beyond the footbridge and you'll soon come to the thundering sight of Aysgill Force.

❻ From the waterfall, continue ahead along the path, all the time keeping the river to your right and following the signs through the series of gates. Eventually you come to a wall and need to turn left, heading up the steep hill. At the top, go through the gate and begin following signs for Gayle once again. You need to go over a small hill before you can see Gayle and the familiar outline of Hawes. At the road, turn right and then at the main road take the turning off to the left. It's easy enough to find as you're following the signs for Hawes. Just after passing the creamery there is a path on the right that takes you across a field and drops down into the town's car park.

18 RIPON
4 miles (6.2 km)

A **great place to spend a day,** the traditional Yorkshire market settlement of Ripon contains many great things to do. Top of the list for dog owners is the lovely walk from the centre of the town out into the countryside by the canal. This will take you beside the water on an accessible, largely flat stroll out to the racecourse and much further if you feel like stretching your legs for longer. Ripon is one of the smallest cities in the country but despite being home to just 16,000 people, it has a magnificent cathedral and a history that goes back 1300 years. People also visit the city to see the UNESCO World Heritage Site at Studley Royal Park and Fountains Abbey, just outside the city.

Start & Finish: The Navigation Inn, Bondgate Green Lane.
Sat Nav: HG4 1QN .
Parking: Street parking is available on the B6265 Bondgate Green or on Bondgate Green Lane near the pub.
OS Map: OS Explorer 299 Ripon & Boroughbridge.
Grid ref: SE315708.

THE PUB Conveniently located close to the start of the Ripon canal, the **NAVIGATION INN** is a good place to grab a pint or sample some of the hearty pub classics on the menu. With a reputation for being a friendly place that welcomes dogs, you can take a seat either inside or outside. ☎ 01765 600030 ⊕ thenavigationripon.co.uk

Terrain: Canal towpath, all on the level.
Livestock: None.
Stiles: No stiles.
Nearest vet: Bishopton Veterinary Group, Mill Farm, Studley Road, Ripon, HG24 2QR ☎ 01765 602396 ⊕ bishoptonvets.co.uk

The Walk

● ●

❶ From the Navigation Inn head back to the main road and turn right. Enter the courtyard on the right opposite Ripon Bowling Club, near the head of the canal, where you'll also find a lovely little café if you need a cuppa before setting off. Proceed towards the canal, sticking to the left side of it and walking by the houses on the left. This is a pleasant and level path that's accessible to all and is popular with people getting in and out of the city as well as those taking their dog for a stroll. It follows the path of the canal as it mirrors Boroughbridge Road and bends to the right.

2 As the roads meet a major roundabout junction, the path by the canal sneaks under a tunnel to keep you away from the bustle. The path continues on an embankment at the side of the canal and leaves the road as it bends to the right and heads downhill slightly as a lock deals with the height problem.

3 Continue ahead and follow the path around on another right-hand bend.

After passing a caravan site on the other side of the water, you'll soon come to the delightful racecourse marina where several boats are moored. This is, as the name suggests, close to Ripon Racecourse.

4 The wonderful waterside walk continues down the left side of the canal. Just after reaching Ripon Boat Club you will walk past another fine marina filled with boats, providing a wonderful feature to sit beside the Yorkshire countryside.

5 When you reach Renton's Bridge further along the canal, the path crosses over to the other side of the canal and continues ahead. Here you have the choice of pressing on and spending longer to take your dog for a walk, or returning back to the pub in Ripon. If you decide to head back, the route follows the simple way back so as to allow maximum off-lead time and give your dog the most freedom. The possibilities for continuing the walk ahead, however, are immense. If you have the appetite for it, there are another 4 miles of canal path heading down to Boroughbridge. Complete as much or as little of this walk as you wish, making this a flexible route to suit all tastes – and weather forecasts!

19 RICHMOND
3½ miles (5.7 km)

A lovely circular walk in the heart of North Yorkshire, this will take you past a historic abbey and along the side of one of the county's best-known rivers. With some of the walk edging close to the River Swale and the return section featuring an old railway track with lots of off-lead time, this is a popular walk amongst dog owners. With astounding views, a wonderful set of landmarks and a thoroughly interesting back story, Richmond has been hailed as one of the most romantic destinations in the north of England. It's certainly a market town you won't regret heading to. Before you go, make sure you check out the story of the Richmond Drummer Boy. When soldiers in the 18th century found a tunnel beneath the castle that was too small for them to enter, they sent in a young drummer boy and asked him to beat his drum so they could follow the noise above ground. The soldiers kept track of the beating drum for three miles, but then it mysteriously stopped. Nobody knows what became of the drummer boy. His story is marked on information boards and a local walk.

Start & Finish: Market Place, Richmond. **Sat Nav: DL10 4QQ.**
Parking: There is a car park in the centre of Richmond in Market Place.
OS Map: OS Explorer 304: Darlington & Richmond.
Grid ref: NZ170008.

THE PUB **THE CASTLE TAVERN**, on Market Place right in the middle of Richmond, is always at the heart of what's going on. Dogs are welcome inside the bar area, which usually hosts a busy mix of locals and tourists. The pub is ideally located, giving you proximity to the Norman castle that gives it a name and it's only a short stroll to the beautiful River Swale. The menu sources food locally when possible, including tarts that are made just a short walk from the bar and award-winning sausages that are perfect for a post-walk treat.
☎ 01748 826931 ⊕ castletavernrichmond.com

Terrain: Well established paths, including a former railway line.
Livestock: Sheep may be encountered on farming fields. Observe local signs.
Stiles: No stiles.
Nearest vet: Swale Veterinary Surgery, Fairfield Way, Richmond, DL10 4TB. ☎ 01748 826600

The Walk

● This pleasant circular walk starts right in the middle of Richmond in the market place. Head down the slope and pass the church until you reach the

road at the bottom. Turn right and you'll be on Millgate, a lovely road that continues down the hill and gives a great view of the castle up on the right.

2 Continue to follow the road until you come to a car park near the River Swale. At the far-left side of the car park, pick up the riverside path that takes you alongside the Swale. This is a lovely part of the walk, with the flowing water and open picnic area providing some much-loved off-lead time. As you come to the bridge over the road, take the path over to the left leading to the road.

3 Cross the road and head down the lane called Lombards Wynd. This takes you on the right-hand side of the churchyard, and then you take the path on the right. This is a popular path that is signed for Easby Abbey and, sure enough, in just under 1 mile you'll be brought out at the abbey site after passing through a small wood.

4 The abbey was founded in 1152 and is an impressive sight in any weather. When you head just beyond it, you'll come to a small road and need to turn right here. When the road splits, take the option on

the left and follow the road as it turns into a track.

5 When this track bends around to the left, take the route on the right that crosses over the Swale via an old iron bridge. You're now following in the footsteps of the railway that used to serve Richmond. You should follow the old railway

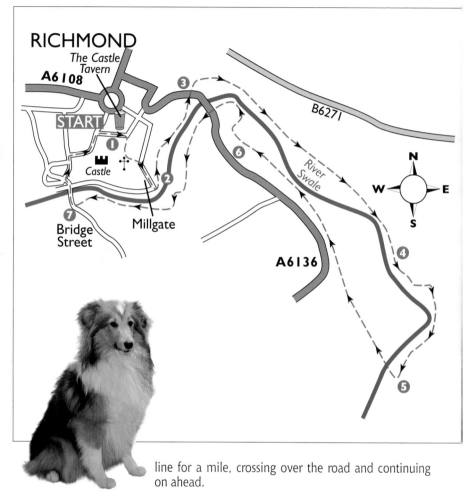

RICHMOND

The Castle Tavern

A6108

START

Castle

Millgate

Bridge Street

B6271

River Swale

A6136

N
W E
S

line for a mile, crossing over the road and continuing on ahead.

6 When you reach the leisure centre, head down the steps to the right of the swimming pool and turn left on the path at the riverside. Follow the signs for the footpath as this sticks to the side of the river, bends around the left and passes under a bridge. There are a few kissing gates to go through. Continue to follow this path, which sticks close to the river and eventually passes Richmond Football Club.

7 When the path brings you to a road in just over ½ mile, turn left onto Bridge Street and cross over the River Swale once more. With the castle looming large on the right, continue ahead and turn right when you reach New Road. This will bring you back to Market Place, where you should turn left to get back to the place where the walk started.

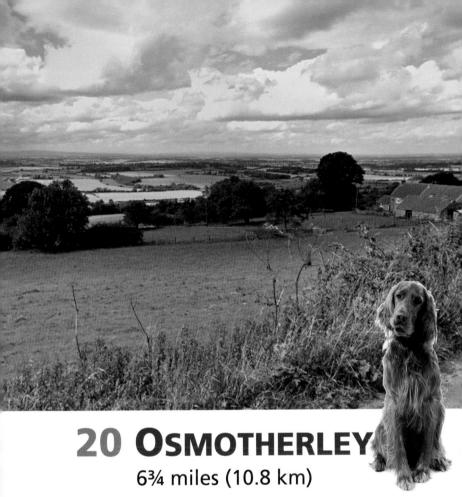

20 OSMOTHERLEY
6¾ miles (10.8 km)

The village green in the middle of Osmotherley is as picturesque a place as you'll find, with pretty houses, a monument and a barter table. The most noticeable aspect of the village's centre, however, is that there are no fewer than three pubs all within 50 metres! If there was ever a place to settle down for the evening after a beautiful walk, then this is it! The circular walk from Osmotherley takes you through woods and by rivers, providing plenty of opportunities for your dog to have a great day out. Some of the route makes up the Cleveland Way, a 110-mile trail that curves in and around the North York Moors on its way from Helmsley to Filey Brigg.

Start & Finish: The Golden Lion, West End.
Sat Nav: DL6 3AG.
Parking: Street parking in the centre of Osmotherley, outside the Golden Lion.
OS Map: OS Explorer OL26 North York Moors, Western Area.
Grid ref: SE456972.

THE PUB Welcoming dogs with open arms, the **GOLDEN LION** at Osmotherley is a family-friendly pub that has centuries of tradition behind it. The inn dates back to the 18th century and inside you'll see many of the original stone features that give it such a quaint feel. The benches to many tables are actually old pews, there's a range of artwork on the walls that depict the local countryside over the seasons and the candlelit tables add to the cosy atmosphere. After the beautiful walk along the edge of the North York Moors, this is the perfect place to come and unwind, warm up and reflect on the day's adventures.

☎ 01609 883526

⊕ goldenlionosmotherley.co.uk

Terrain: Well-established footpaths, with some small climbs and places that can be muddy after rain.
Livestock: None.
Stiles: No stiles.
Nearest vet: Forrest House Veterinary Group, 51 Stokesley Road, Brompton, Northallerton, DL6 2TS.
☎ 01609 778200 ⊕ forresthouse-veterinary.co.uk

The Walk

1 Set off from the centre of Osmotherley, where the Golden Lion overlooks the village green. As you face the pub, walk off to the right and proceed up North End, passing the church on your right. Continue straight ahead on the road, leaving the middle of the village behind you.

2 Turn left when you reach Ruebury Lane and walk on this small country lane as it passes houses and enters the countryside with farms on either side. This is the Cleveland Way, which bends away to the right when it reaches Chapelwood Farm and starts to climb the hill. The views really start to open up as you climb, so keep having a look around you.

3 The path forks just before entering Arncliffe Wood and you need to stick to the Cleveland Way, taking the option on the right. The path runs straight at this point and is easy to follow, climbing the hill and leaving the woods. You'll pass a telecommunication station on the left. This is a delightful section of the walk, with some good off-lead

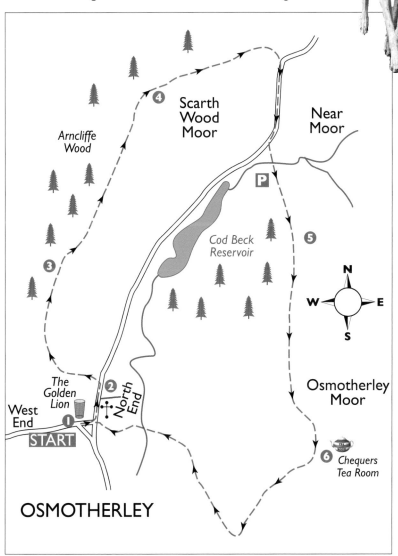

time for the dogs as you pass through wooded areas and follow the path next to a drystone wall on the right. Pass a trig point on the right and you'll soon come to a junction of paths.

4 Continue to follow the Cleveland Way as it takes you out onto the exposed moorland and allows you to enjoy views of the iconic Roseberry Topping in the distance. This track is easy to follow and soon takes a dramatic swing to the right, beginning a steady descent down towards the road. Turn right here and walk down the country road towards the Cod Beck Reservoir car park. Just before you reach it, however, the road bends sharply to the right and you should take the wide track that rises up over the moors once more.

5 This well-established track, once used by drovers to move their sheep, takes you next to a small plantation and proceeds over the moors until it brings you out at a small road in ¾ mile. Turn left here and you'll soon come to a tea room that's a lovely place to get some refreshments and enjoy the views.

6 Just beyond Chequers Tea Room, take the path on the right that starts to lead down the hill once more. Keep going for around ¾ mile until, at

the bottom, this path bends around to the left and joins the Cleveland Way once more. Turn right here and you will head back into Osmotherley. If you keep following the signs for the Cleveland Way as it crosses over the fields, you'll find yourself, after 1¼ miles, arriving back into the middle of the village.

A SELECTION OF OTHER DOG FRIENDLY COUNTRY PUBS IN NORTH YORKSHIRE

Aldborough – The Ship Inn
Aldwark – Aldwark Arms
Anderby Steeple – Wellington Heifer
Austwick – The Traddock Hotel
Bagby – Bagby Inn
Bedale – The Green Dragon, The Bay Horse Inn, The Greyhound Inn
Boroughbridge – The Crown Inn, The Dunsforth
Easingwold – The Angel
East Cowton – The Beeswing Inn
East Witton – Blue Lion, Cover Bridge Inn
Goathland – The Station Tavern
Great Ayton – Royal Oak
Harmby – The Pheasant Inn
Hawes – White Hart Inn, Crown Hotel
Helperby – Oak Tree Inn
Husthwaite – Plum and Partridge

Kilburn – The Forresters Arms
Leyburn – The Leyburn Bolton Arms, Black Swan, The Sandpiper
Malham – The Buck Inn
Masham – White Bear, Kings Head Hotel
Middleham – Black Swan
Northallerton – Golden Lion, The Standard, The Green Tree Inn
Osmotherley – The Thee Tuns Inn, Queen Catherine Hotel
Rainton – The Lamb Inn
Riccall – The Drovers Arms
Richmond – White Cross, The Marlborough, Lass O'Richmond Hill
Ripon – The Water Rat, One Eyed Rat, The Royal Oak, The Golden Lion
Skelton on Ure – Black Lion
Snape – The Castle Arms Inn
Thirsk – Frankland Arms, Little 3, Black lion, Old Oak Tree
Whitby – The Endeavour, Little Angel, The Granby, The Fleece
York – The Punch Bowl